KT-422-463

Feng Shaun

Discover Inner Peace with Shaun the Sheep

First published 2002 by Boxtree
an imprint of Pan Macmillan Ltd
Pan Macmillan, 20 New Wharf Road, London N1 9RR
Basingstoke and Oxford
Associated companies throughout the world
www.panmacmillan.com

ISBN 0 7522 1512 4

Produced under license by Aardman Animations
© and ™ Aardman/Wallace and Gromit Ltd 2002

Text © Macmillan Publishers Ltd 2002

All rights reserved. No part of this publication may be reproduced, stored in or introduced into a retrieval system, or transmitted, in any form, or by any means (electronic, mechanical, photocopying, recording or otherwise) without the prior written permission of the publisher. Any person who does any unauthorized act in relation to this publication may be liable to criminal prosecution and civil claims for damages.

5 7 9 8 6 4

A CIP catalogue record for this book is available from
the British Library.

Design by Dan Newman, Perfect Bound
Text by Natalie Jerome and Emma Marriott

Printed by Proost, Belgium

Feng Shaun

Discover Inner Peace with Shaun the Sheep

BOXTREE

Wear white, natural fabrics to induce a feeling of calm and purity

CLEAR AWAY CLUTTER

Clutter blocks vital energy, leading to frustration and subtle obstacles in your life

Spending more time in good company and less time in bad company will have a positive effect on your mental and spiritual wellbeing

Slow, repetitive tasks are a great way to ease an anxious mind

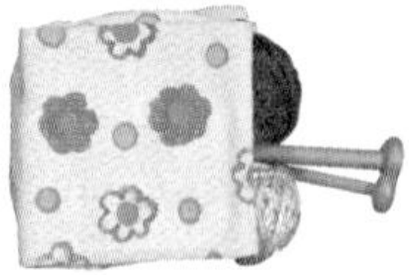

Introduce love into your life – it has a positive affect on your thinking patterns and endorphin levels

Prayer is often the only solution to certain insurmountable problems

LOOK GOOD, FEEL GREAT!

Personal grooming is essential for increasing self-esteem. Make sure you look your very best every day

Understand your cravings and addictions – they show a lack of control and cause unhappiness

One of the surest ways of soothing anxiety is through touch. An arm on a shoulder is a simple gesture that can sometimes work wonders

Even basic Tai Chi can lead to instant feelings of calm

After a hard day, there's nothing better than a good long soak to revive and refresh that tired old body

Remember to take every opportunity to inject some passion into your relationship. It will do wonders for body and soul

UNDER PRESSURE

Try not to over-react in times of stress

If in doubt, run away from trouble. Exercise is a great way of alleviating tension

JUST LEAVE ME ALONE!

There comes a time when you need to protect and barricade yourself from potentially stressful situations

IRRITABLE BOWEL?

If you're feeling bloated and gassy, watch your diet. A sore tummy is often due to rich and fatty foods

BE OPEN-MINDED

Make friends with new people. Look beyond appearances and remember, strangers are just friends we haven't met

Eat more greenery – it's the perfect snack food for body and soul

Dealing with anxiety in a calm, dignified manner nourishes your inner self

LIMIT YOUR CAFFEINE INTAKE

Between four and six cups of coffee or tea a day and you are over your caffeine limit. Too much caffeine can make you hyperactive

TO ERR IS HUMAN, TO FORGIVE DIVINE

Anger is a negative emotion – be bigger than your enemies and forgive others as often as you can

BREATHE DEEPLY

When feeling pressured, breathe in slowly through the nose and out through the mouth. You will soon begin to feel relaxed

AND FINALLY . . .

Read this book as often as you can – on the bus, on the tube or train, in a quiet field . . . whenever you feel your blood starting to boil, your stress levels rising and your hands forming a fist.

Remember your pal Shaun is there for you – don't forget the simple tenets of his wisdom and . . .

JUST TAKE IT EASY!